MEL BAY'S
Irish Session Tune Book

Over 300 Favorite Session Tunes

Arranged Alphabetically by Name within Type

(140 Reels; 98 Jigs; 29 Hornpipes; 45 Polkas, Slides & Slip-Jigs)

Collected, Transcribed & Edited by

Cari Fuchs

Cover Credit: The Slide File, Ireland

Visit us on the Web at http://www.melbay.com — E-mail us at email@melbay.com

June, 1996

Introduction

The dance music of Ireland constitutes a living <u>oral</u> tradition. The tunes in this collection were largely learned by ear, with the help of a small portable tape recorder. The great majority were acquired over the past 5-10 years at Irish sessions in Boston, Pittsburgh, West Virginia (at the Augusta Heritage Program's Irish Week), and elsewhere in my travels (including Ireland). I would like to thank the many fine and dedicated musicians, particularly my daughter, the New England fiddler Viveka Fox, who generously shared tunes and tips with me, and gave me so many hours of pleasure in playing this music. Where feasible, I have double-checked tunes against recordings by well-known Irish musicians and other printed collections.

This book is meant to serve the various melodic instruments played in Irish sessions. I have attempted to notate the ornamentations and variations that are so intrinsic to this music, and give it such joy and life. However, these ornaments are played differently depending on the instrument and region. The reader should feel free to change ornaments and variations to suit his/her individual style and instrument (using whatever notes are easiest to finger), without obscuring the melody and lilt of the tune. This demands that the aspiring player listen a great deal to both recordings and other session musicians. It is traditional at Irish sessions to play in tight unison with the other musicians, adapting appropriate tempos, rhythms, and ornaments in an attempt to fit in with the "groove."

In transcribing this music I have indicated the usual ornaments and where they might be utilized. Since each tune is written out only once, I have had to show all the possible embellishments simultaneously, in a composite transcription. However, these would never all be played on the same repetition of the tune! Variations in settings are shown either in the repeat of a phrase within the tune, and/or as a second melody line on the same staff. That is, wherever double notes appear, these are not chords but an alternative rendition of the phrase. Where necessary I have marked which time to play which variant; e.g. "1st X" means first time through the part. I have placed parenthesis around notes that can be left out to vary a phrase. The reader is best advised to pick and choose among the many notated embellishments and variations, utilizing just a few of the different settings each time through the tune.

For ease of reading, I have not notated the single grace note, frequently used as a cut to separate two notes of the same pitch. These cuts may be inserted according to the reader's taste. Examples of location of grace notes follow.

Typical insertions of grace notes (cuts):

Throughout this book ornaments are notated
as shown in the table below:

Ornament	**Notation**	**Ways of Playing**

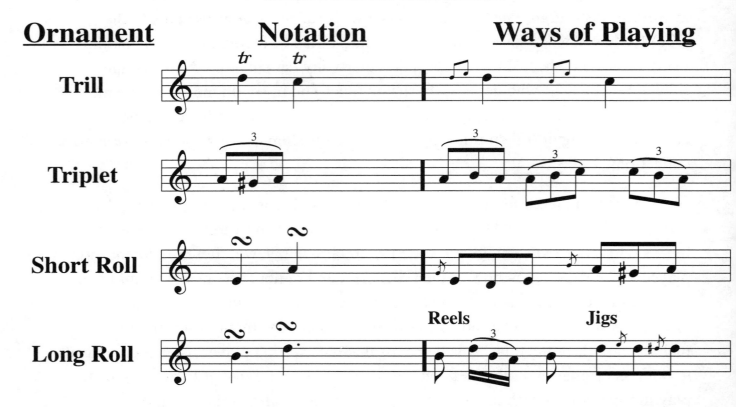

Especially in reels, the 5 notes of a long roll go by so quickly
that it is usually better to just play a triplet.

Roll notes are determined not by key signature, but by
fingering patterns of the instrument. The chart below shows the
use of accidentals in the most common rolls.

Best wishes for great playing!

Cari

Reels

Ah Surely

Atlantic Wave

Martin Mulhaire

Bank of Ireland

Bare Island

Finbar Dwy

Bells of Tipperary

Boy in the Boat

Boil the Breakfast Early
(Peador's)

Boil the Breakfast Medley
(Knocknagow)

The Boyne Hunt

9

Boys of Ballisodare

Boys of the Lough

2nd B Part Optional:
Repeat lst B instead (with A ending)

Bucks of Oranmore

The Cameronian

Castle Kelly

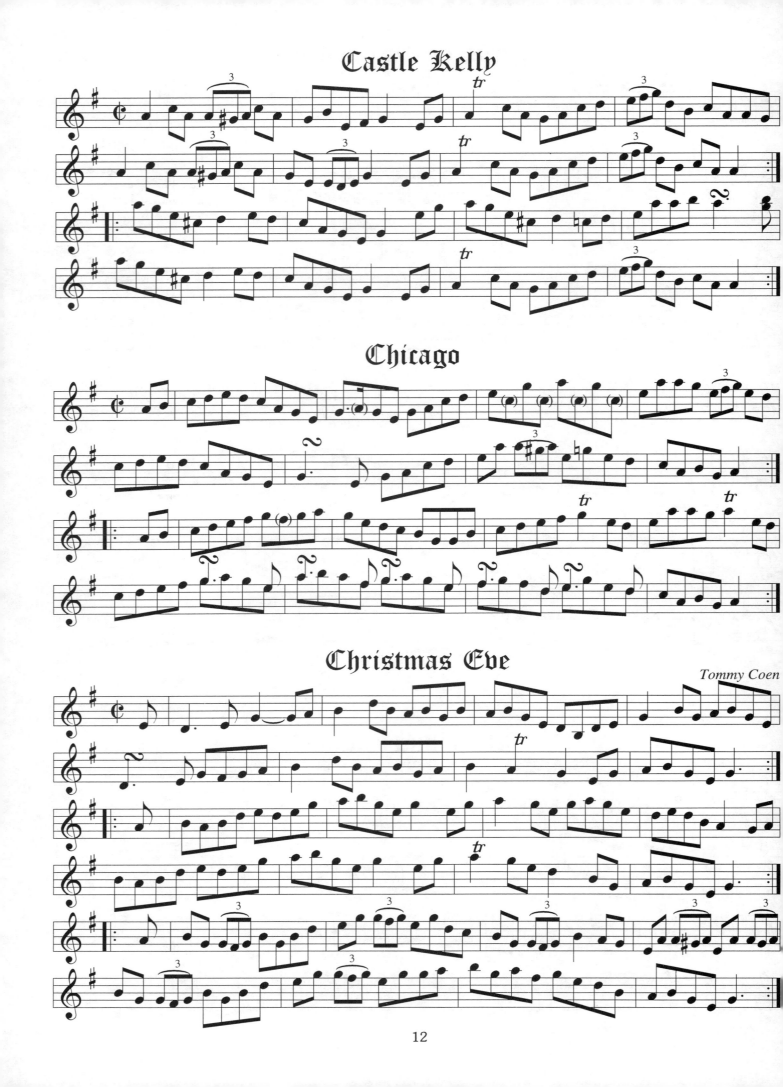

Chicago

Christmas Eve

Tommy Coen

Concertina Reel

Congress

Connamara Stocking
(Galway Reel)

Convenience Reel

Crowley's

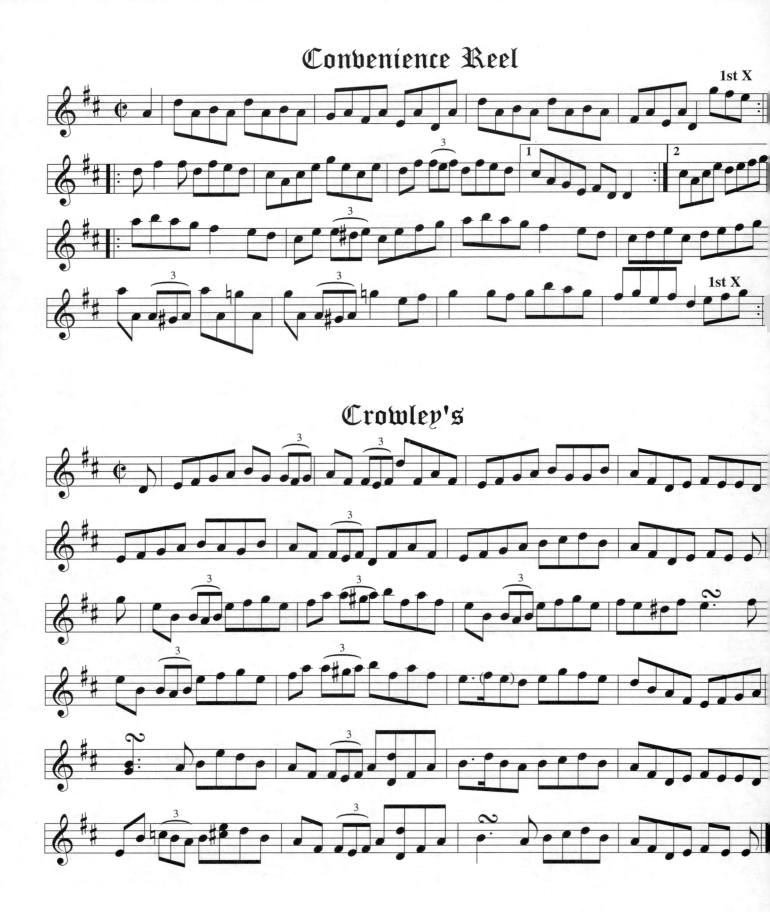

Cup of Tea

Dick Gossip's

Dinky's

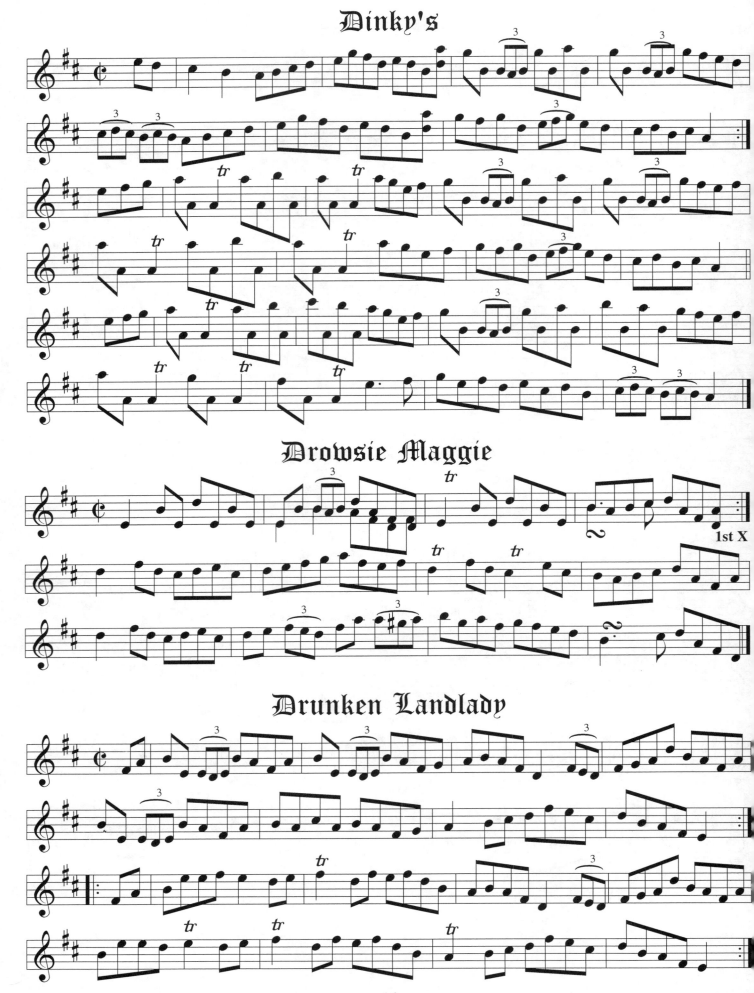

Drowsie Maggie

Drunken Landlady

16

Dublin Reel

(Jackson's)

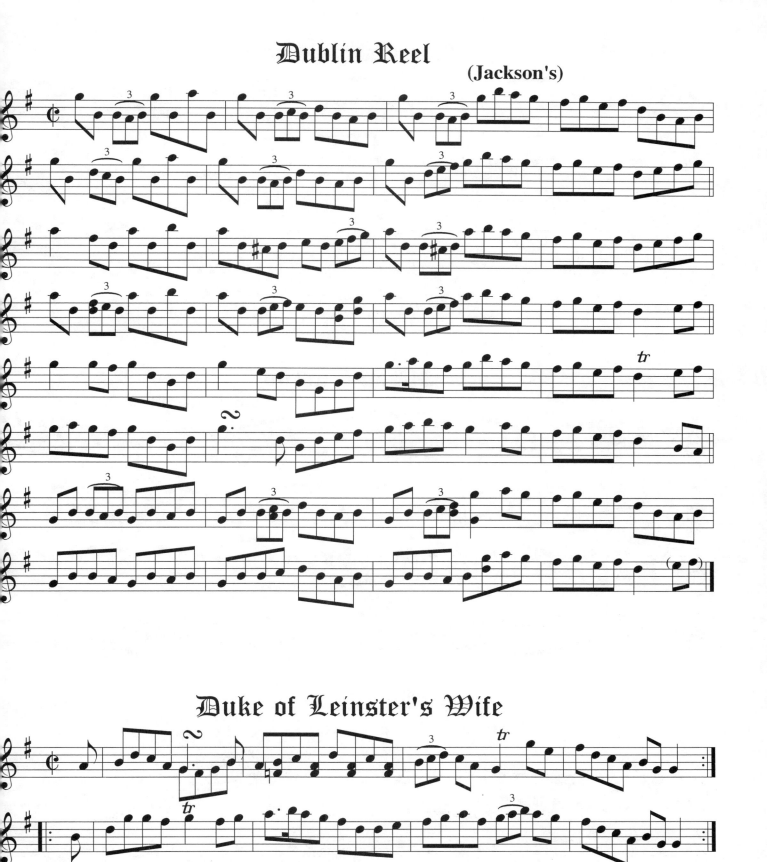

Duke of Leinster's Wife

The Earl's Chair

Eileen Curran
(Sailors Return)

Fahy's

Fairy Reel

Farewell to Connaught

Father Kelly's

Father Kelly's Too

Fermoy Lasses

First House of Connaught

Foxhunter's

Fred Finn's

Glass of Beer

21

Glen Allen

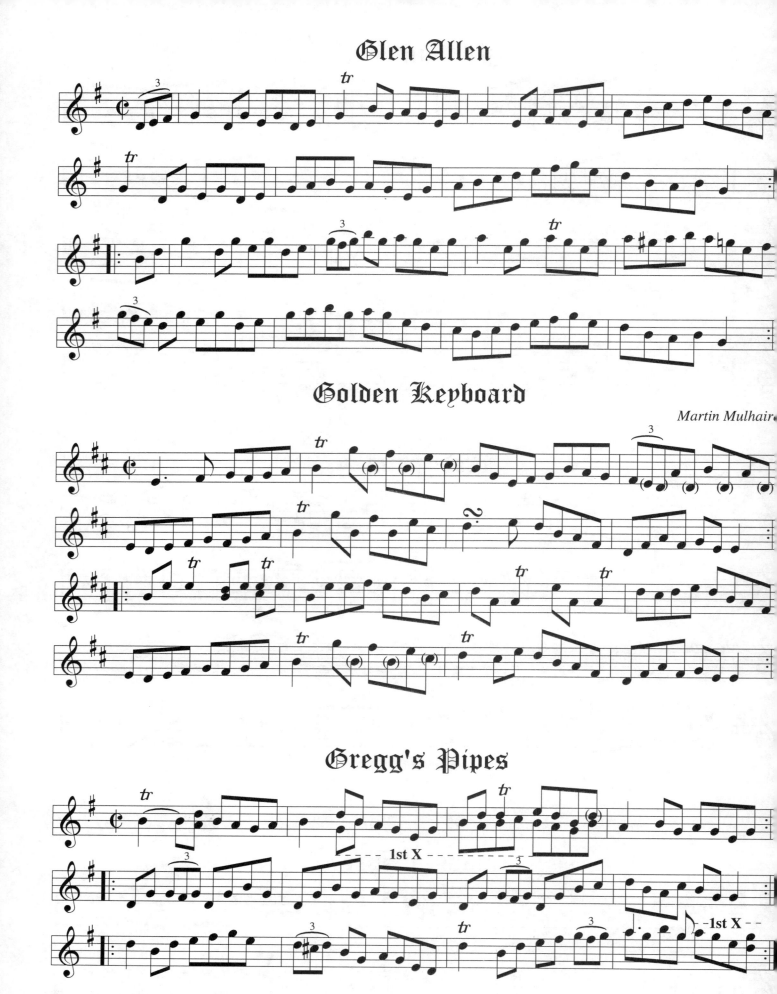

Golden Keyboard

Martin Mulhair

Gregg's Pipes

Gravel Walk

Greenfields of America

23

Heather Breeze

1st X

High Reel

High Reel Too

High Road to Linton

Humours of Tulla

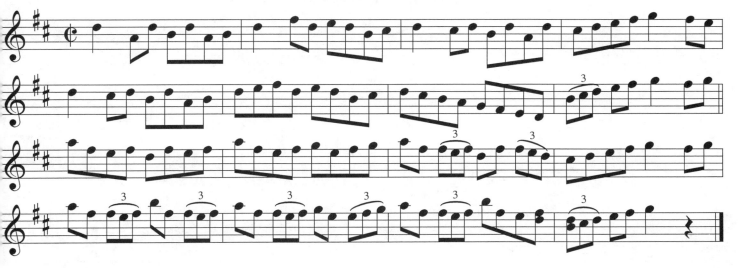

Humours of Westport

Hunter's Purse

Jackie Coleman's

Jackson's

*Substitute Turn-Around

*Turn-Around:
(Substitute for 1st measure)

Jenny's Chickens

(Sleepy Maggie)

4th Part Optional

Joe Cooley's

John Bowes

John Brennan's

John Dwyer's

Julia Delaney

28

Kathleen Brennan

Keith Murphy

Viveka Fox

Killarney Boys of Pleasure

29

Killavil Fancy
(10 Pound Float)

Killfodda

Larry Redican

Knotted Cord

Kitty's Gone a-Milking

Lady Anne Montgomery

Longford Tinker

(Jenny Dang the Weaver)

Lucy Campbell

Maid Behind the Bar

Maid of Mt. Kisco

Maids of Castlebar

Mamma's Pet

33

Martin Wynne's

Martin Wynne's Too

Mason's Apron

Master Crowley

McDermott's

McMahon's
(the Banshee)

Miss Johnson

Miss McLeod

Miss Monaghan

Morning Dew

Mountain Road

Michael Gorman

3rd Part Optional

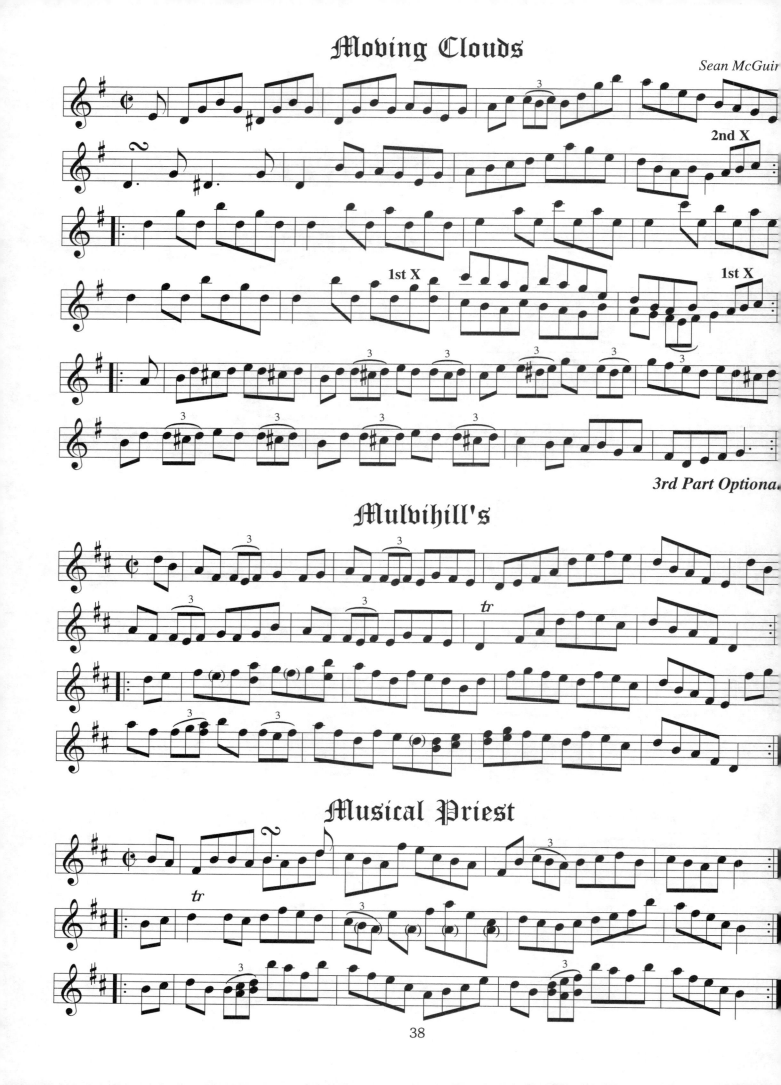

Moving Clouds

Sean McGuir...

2nd X

1st X   **1st X**

3   3   3   3

3   3   3   3

3rd Part Optiona...

Mulvihill's

tr

Musical Priest

tr

Nine Points of Roguery

O'Rourkes

Old Bush

Repeat B part here

39

Over the Moor to Maggie

Paddy on the Railroad

(Merry Blacksmith)

Paddy on the Turnpike

Paddy's Trip to Scotland

Peter Street

Pigeon on the Gate

Pinch of Snuff

Primrose Lass

Providence

Rakish Paddy

Redican's

(Galway)

1st X

Reel of Mullinavat

Return to Miltown

1st X

Road to Rio

Sean Ryan

Sailor on the Rock

Salamanca

The Scholar

3 Part Variations

Sally Gardens

Sean Ryan's

Sergeant Early's Dream

Shannon Breeze

(Rolling on the Ryegrass)

Shaskeen

2nd Ending Optional

Sheehan's

Sheila Coyles

Ships are Sailing

Silver Spear

Silver Spire

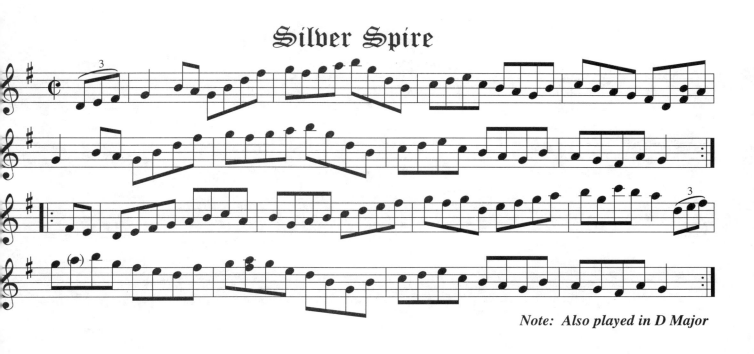

Note: Also played in D Major

The Skylark

Sligo Maid

Sporting Nell

Star of Munster

Stoney Steps

Swallowtail

Sweeney's Wheel

Jackie Daly

Sweeney's Dream

Swinging on a Gate

Tarbolton

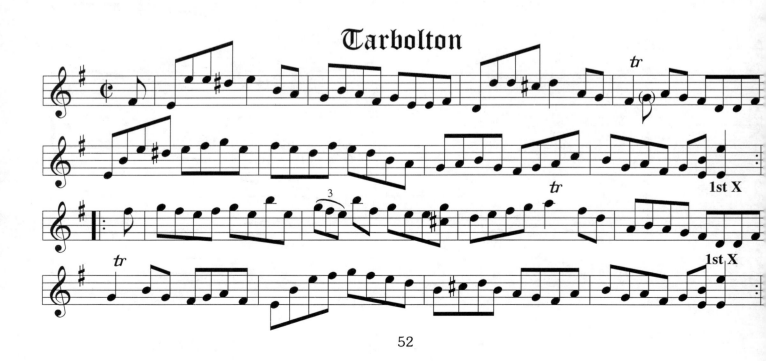

52

Tam Lin

(Glasgow Reel; Howling Wind)

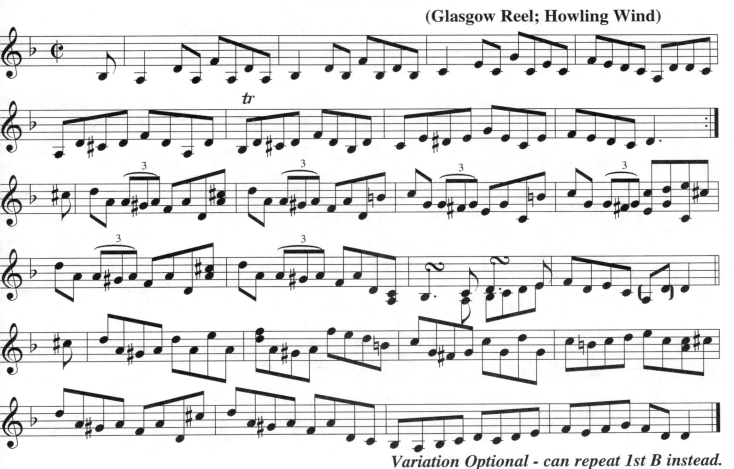

Variation Optional - can repeat 1st B instead.

Alternate Setting

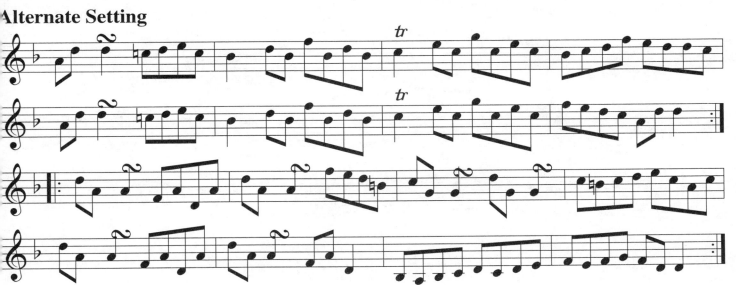

Note: Tune often repeated in A Minor

Tear the Calico

Temperance Reel
(Teetotaler's)

Toss the Feathers

Tom Billy's

(Speed the Plough)

Touch Me If You Dare

The Traveller

(The Carpenter)

Trim the Velvet

Trip to Durrow

Wise Maid

Woman of the House

Yellow Tinker

57

Andy DeJarlis

Andy McGann's

Banish Misfortune

Behind the Haystack

(Munster Buttermilk)

Bank of Turf

Banks of Lough Gowna

Behind the Bush in the Garden

Blackthorn Stick

1st X

Blarney Pilgrim

Boys of the Town

Burnt Old Man

Butcher's

Carraroe

Cliffs of Moher

Coleraine

Con Cassidy

Connaughtman's Rambles

Contentment is Wealth

Crabs in the Skillet

Dan Dowd's

Dancing Tables

Liz Carroll

Donneybrook Fair

(Joys of My Life)

Dr. O'Neill

Eavesdropper

70

The Gallowglass

Gander in the Pratie Hole

Geese in the Bog

The Gobby, O

Gold Ring

Haste to the Wedding

High Part of the Road

Irish Washerwoman

73

Humours of Ballyloughlin

An Irishman's Heart to the Ladies

Humours of Ennistymon

Jordan Farm

Viveka Fox

Jig of Slurs

Kesh

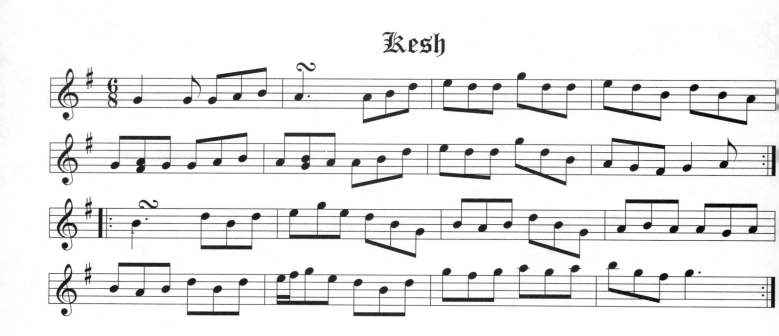

Lad O'Beirne's

(Returned Yank; Racoon Cap)

Lannigan's Ball

Lark on the Strand

Langstrom's Pony

Larry O'Gaff

(Daniel O'Connell)

Lark in the Morning

Leitrum Fancy

Lilting Banshee
(Paddy Ryan's Favorite)

The Master's Return

McDermitt's Fancy

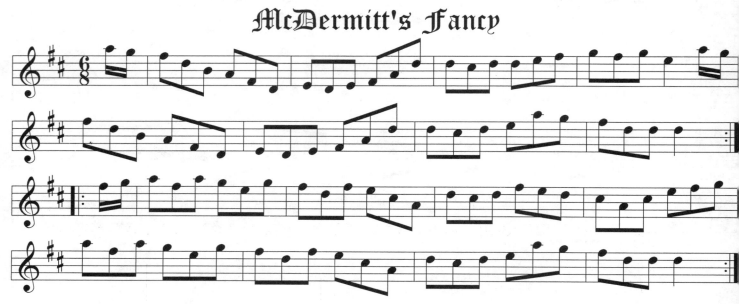

Maggie Brown's

Maid at the Spinning Wheel

Merrily Kiss the Quaker's Wife

Mist on the Mountain

Morrison's

Mug of Brown Ale

(Clare Jig)

Munster Buttermilk

Old Hag You Have Killed Me

Old Man Dillon

Old Grey Goose

Old Woman Tossed Up in a Blanket

Out on the Ocean

Paddy Clancy's

Paddy Fahy's

Palm Sunday

Patsy Geary's

Pay the Reckoning

(Jackson's Bottle of Brandy)

Pipe on the Hob

Richard Brennan's

Rakes of Clonmel

Last 2 parts rarely played; B part repeated instead of variation.

Rakes of Kildare

Rambling Pitchfork
(Fisherman's Widow)

1st X

Rambling Pitchfork Too

Road to Lisdoonvarna

Rolling Waves

Rose in the Heather

Saddle the Pony

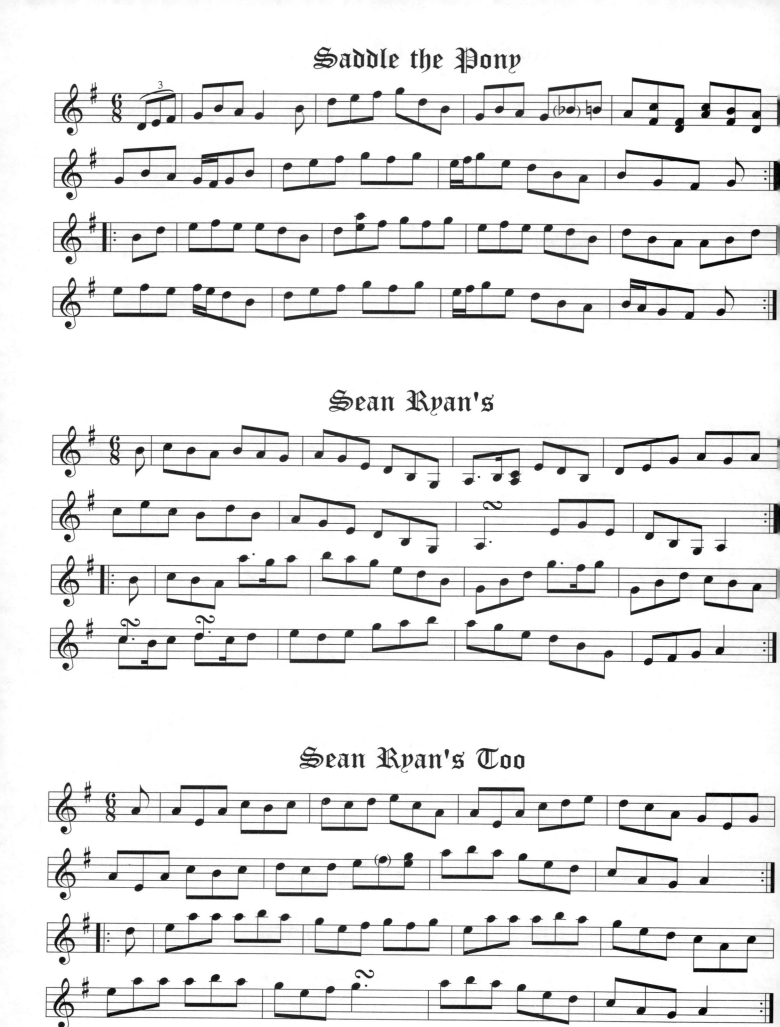

Sean Ryan's

Sean Ryan's Too

92

Shannon Bells

Slieve Russel

Snug in the Blanket

Smash the Windows
(Roaring Jelly)

Swedish Jig
(Arthur Darley's)

Sporting Pitchfork

Tar Road to Sligo

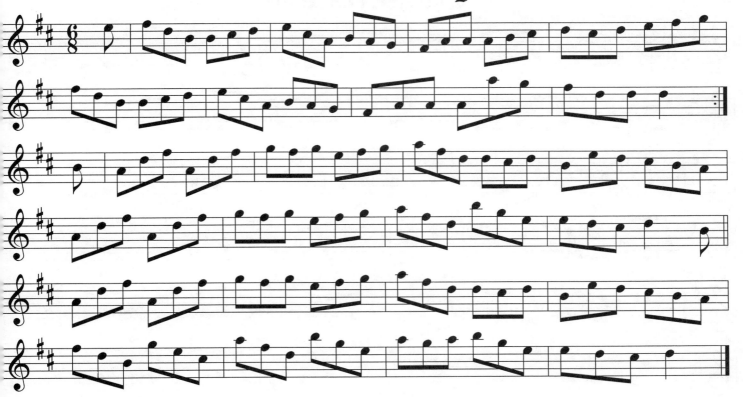

Tea Song
(Cul Aodha)

Tell Her I Am

1st X

Tenpenny Bit

Tobin's Favorite

Tom Billy's

Tom Billy Murphy

Tongs by the Fire

Top of Cork Road

Trip to Athlone

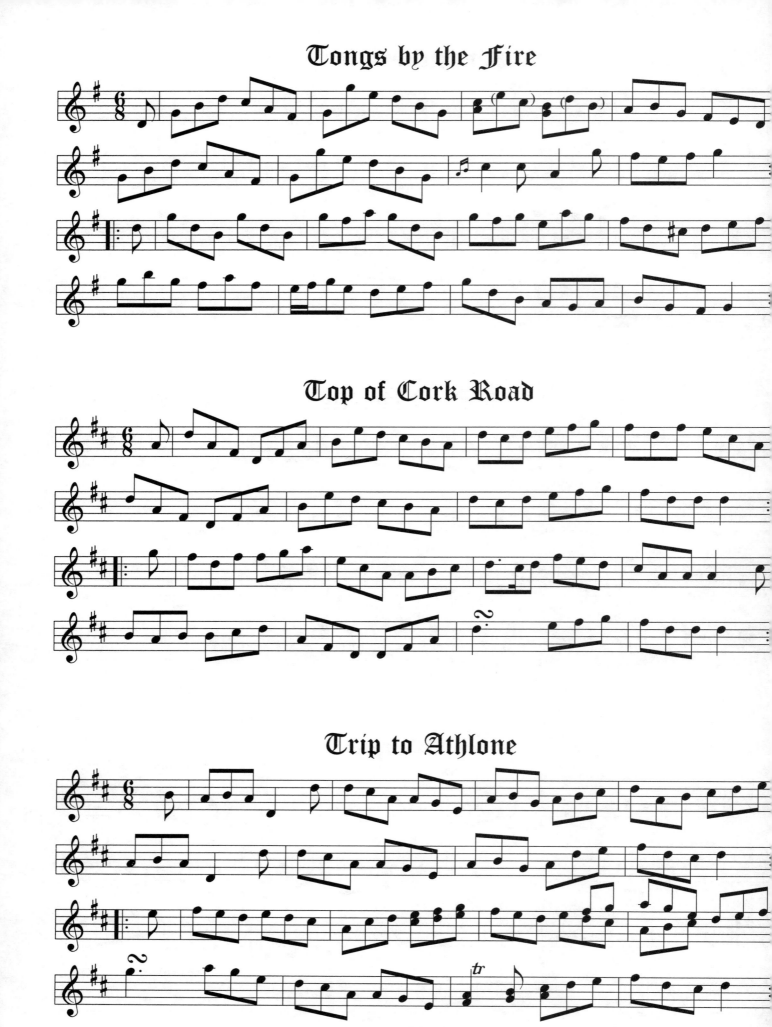

Trip to Sligo

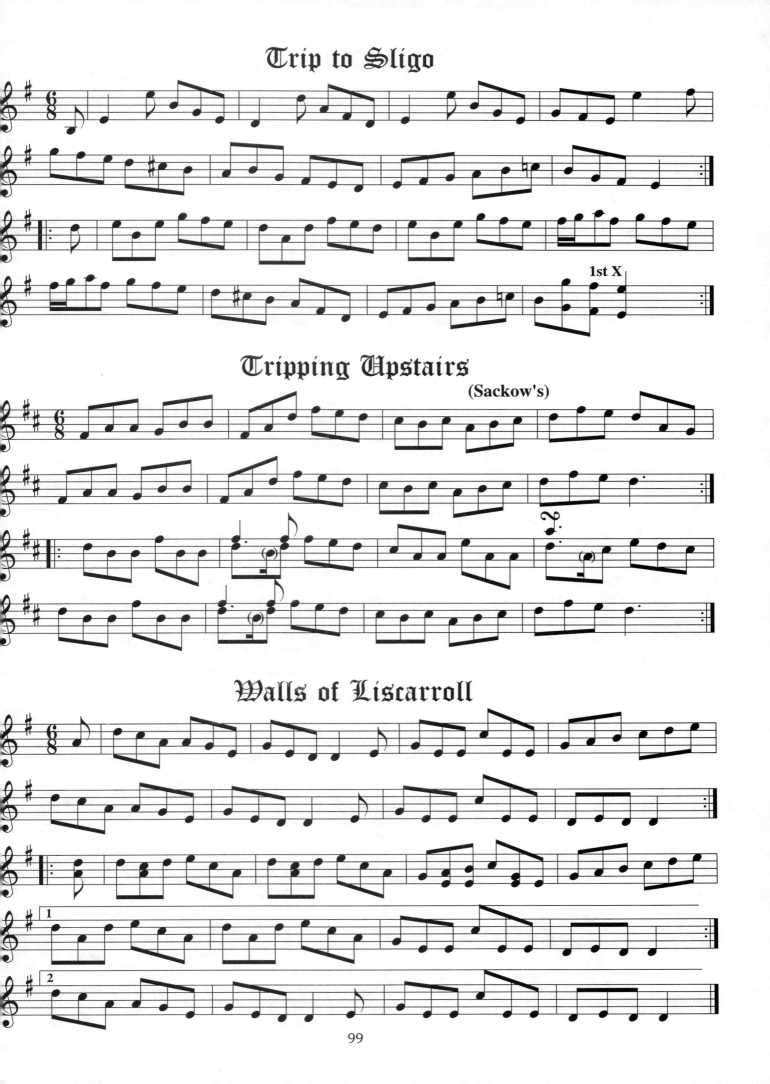

Tripping Upstairs

(Sackow's)

Walls of Liscarroll

99

West Clare Jig

(Bush on the Hill)

When Sick Is It Tea You Want?

Willy Coleman's

Hornpipes

Note: The dotted rhythm shown in the first measure of each hornpipe should be used throughout the tune.

Alexander's

Belfast

Boys of Bluehill

Durang's

First of May

103

Fisher's

2nd X

Flowers of Edinburgh

Flowing Tide

From Galway to Dublin

Galway

Galway Bay

Golden Eagle

Green Grow the Rushes

Harvest Home

106

Home Ruler

Kildare Fancy

Kitty's Wedding

Liverpool

The Mountain Top

Off to California

Paddy O'Brien's

Plains of Boyle

Poppy Leaf

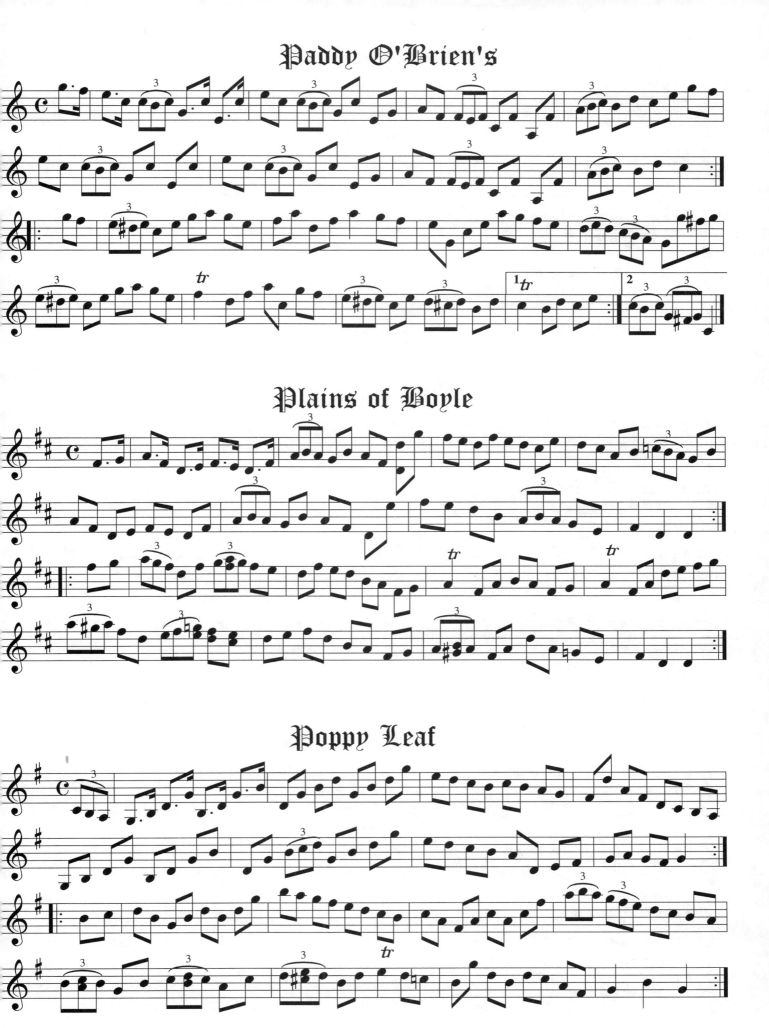

The Reconciliation

Rights of Man

Showman's Fancy

Spellan the Fiddler

Stack of Barley

Stack of Wheat

Polkas, Slides & Slip-Jigs

Polkas

Balleydesmond Polkas

Denis Murphy

Ned Connell

Denis Murphy

Ballyvournie Polka

Banks of Inverness

Britches Full of Stitches

Bruce's
(Fred Rice's)

Captain Byng

Charlie Harris

1st X

Finnish

tr

Jessica's

Mick Hanly

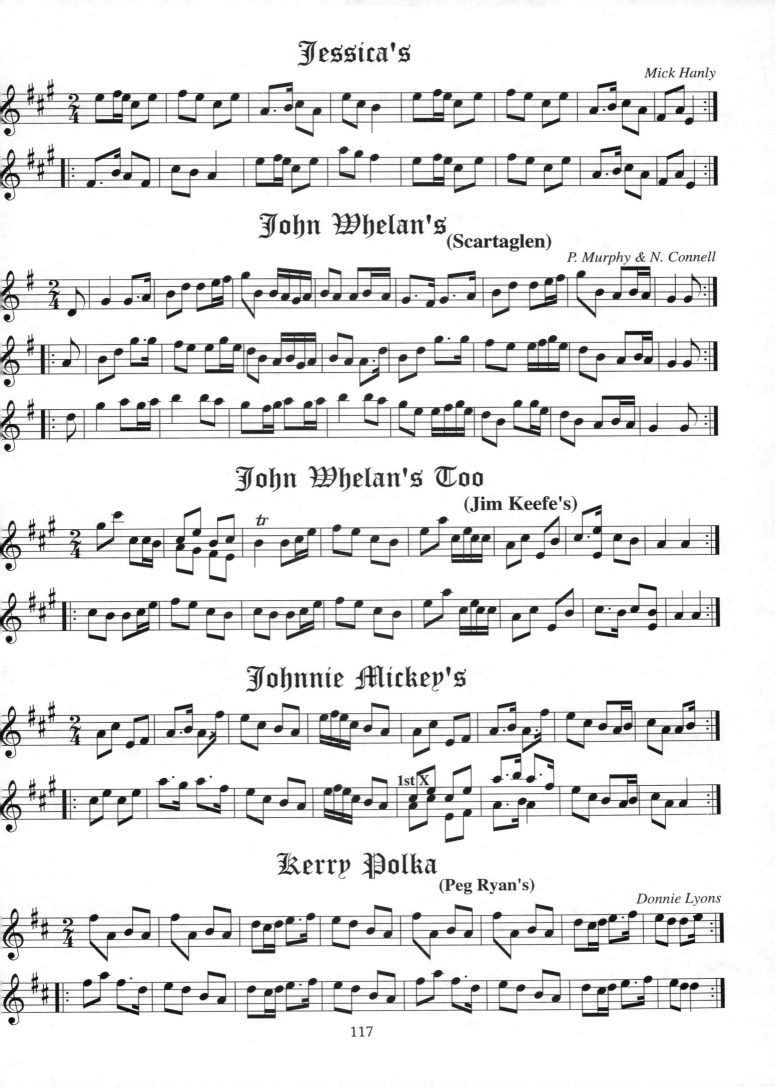

John Whelan's (Scartaglen)

P. Murphy & N. Connell

John Whelan's Too

(Jim Keefe's)

Johnnie Mickey's

Kerry Polka

(Peg Ryan's)

Donnie Lyons

Killavil Postman

Leather Away the Wattle-O

Maggie in the Woods

Maid in the Blue Bonnet

Tommy O'Connor

118

Maid of Ardagh

Micky Chewing Bubblegum

Newmarket

(Art O'Keefe's)

1st X

Ray's Favorite

Richard's

(1.42 lb. Check)

Ryan's

Scottish Polkas

St. Mary's

Church St.

Sweeney's

(Dennis Murphy's)

Slides

Chicago Slide

Connie Walsh's Slide

Dear Lisa
(Have a Drink With Me)

Denis Murphy's Slide

Dingle Regatta

Going to the Well for Water

O'Keefe's Slide

Off She Goes

Slip-Jigs

Boys of Ballysadare

The Butterfly

Dusty Miller

Foxhunter's

Hardiman the Fiddler

Kid on the Mountain

The Parish Jig

Viveka Fox

The Swaggering Jig

(Give Us A Drink)

Whinny Hills of Leitrim

Index of Tunes

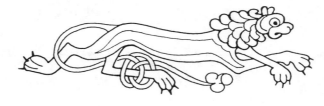

Name	Key*	Type	Name	Key*	Type
Ah Surely	G	Reel	Connaughtman's Rambles	b	Jig
Alexander's	D	Hornpipe	Connamara Stocking	G	Reel
Andy DeJarlis	E	Jig	Connie Walsh's	D	Slide
Andy McGann's	D	Jig	Contentment is Wealth	e	Jig
Atlantic Wave	G	Reel	Convenience	D	Reel
Balleydesmond	D/a$_m$/a$_m$	Polkas	Crabs in the Skillet	g	Jig
Ballyvournie	e$_m$	Polka	Crowley's	e$_m$	Reel
Banish Misfortune	D$_m$	Jig	Cup of Tea	D	Reel
Bank of Ireland	D$_m$	Reel	Dan Dowd's	a$_m$	Jig
Bank of Turf	D	Jig	Dancing Tables	A	Jig
Banks of Inverness	D	Polka	Dear Lisa	G	Slide
Banks of Lough Gowna	f	Jig	Denis Murphy's	D	Slide
Bare Island	e$_m$	Reel	Dick Gossip's	D	Reel
Behind the Bush in the Garden	a	Jig	Dingle Regatta	G	Slide
Behind the Haystack	D	Jig	Dinky's	A$_m$	Reel
Belfast	D	Hornpipe	Donneybrook Fair	G	Jig
Bells of Tipperary	D	Reel	Dr. O'Neill	D	Jig
Blackthorn Stick	G	Jig	Drowsie Maggie	e$_m$	Reel
Blarney Pilgrim	D$_m$	Jig	Drunken Landlady	D$_m$	Reel
Boil the B'kfst Early	D$_m$/a$_m$	Reels	Dublin	G	Reel
Boy in the Boat	D	Reel	Duke of Leinster's Wife	G	Reel
Boyne Hunt	D	Reel	Durang's	D	Hornpipe
Boys of Ballisodare	D$_m$	Reel	Dusty Miller	A	Slip-jig
Boys of Ballysadare	G	Slipjig	Earl's Chair	b	Reel
Boys of Bluehill	D	Hornpipe	Eavesdropper	A	Jig
Boys of the Lough	D	Reel	Eileen Curran	g	Reel
Boys of the Town	G	Jig	Fahy's	d	Reel
Britches Full of Stitches	D$_m$	Polka	Fairy	G	Reel
Bruce's (Fred Rice's)	G	Polka	Farewell to Connaught	D$_m$	Reel
Bucks of Oranmore	A$_m$	Reel	Father Kelly's I&II	G/G	Reels
Burnt Old Man	D	Jig	Fermoy Lasses	G	Reel
Butcher's	G	Jig	Finnish	b	Polka
Butterfly	G	Slip-jig	First House of Connaught	G	Reel
Cameronian	D	Reel	First of May	A$_m$	Hornpipe
Capt. Byng	G	Polka	Fisher's	D	Hornpipe
Carraroe	D	Jig	Flowers of Edinburgh	G	Hornpipe
Castle Kelly	a$_m$	Reel	Flowing Tide	G	Hornpipe
Charlie Harris	D	Polka	Foxhunter's	D	Slip-jig
Chicago	a$_m$	Reel	Foxhunter's	G	Reel
Chicago	G	Slide	Fred Finn	D	Reel
Christmas Eve	G	Reel	From Galway to Dublin	e$_m$	Hornpipe
Cliffs of Moher	a	Jig	Gallowglass	a$_m$	Jig
Coleraine	a	Jig	Galway	D	Hornpipe
Con Cassidy	GD	Jig	Galway Bay	e	Hornpipe
Concertina	D	Reel	Gander in the Pratie Hole	D$_m$	Jig
Congress	a$_m$	Reel	Geese in the Bog	a$_m$	Jig

Glass of Beer	D	Reel		Leitrum Fancy	G	Jig
Glen Allen	G	Reel		Lilting Banshee	a$_m$	Jig
Gobby, O	a$_m$	Jig		Liverpool	D	Hornp.
Going to the Well for Water	D	Slide		Longford Tinker	b	Reel
Gold Ring	D	Jig		Lucy Campbell	D	Reel
Golden Keyboard	e$_m$	Reel		Maggie Brown's	G	Jig
Golden Eagle	G	Hornpipe		Maggie in the Woods	G	Polka
Gravel Walk	a$_m$	Reel		Maid at the Spinning Wheel	G	Jig
Green Grow the Rushes	G	Hornpipe		Maid Behind the Bar	D	Reel
Greenfields of America	G	Reel		Maid in the Blue Bonnet	D	Polka
Gregg's Pipes	G	Reel		Maid of Ardagh	DA	Polka
Hardiman the Fiddler	a$_m$	Slip-jig		Maid of Mt. Kisco	a$_m$	Reel
Harvest Home	D	Hornpipe		Maids of Castlebar	D	Reel
Haste to the Wedding	D	Jig		Mamma's Pet	G	Reel
Heather Breeze	G	Reel		Martin Wynne's I & II	D/b	Reels
High I & II	A$_m$/D	Reels		Mason's Apron	A	Reel
High Part of the Road	G	Jig		Master Crowley	d$_m$	Reel
High Road to Linton	A	Reel		Master's Return	D	Jig
Home Ruler	D	Hornpipe		McDermitt's Fancy	D	Jig
Humours of Ballyloughlin	D$_m$	Jig		McDermott's	D	Reel
Humours of Ennistymon	G	Jig		McMahon's	G	Reel
Humours of Tulla	D	Reel		Merrily Kiss the Quaker's Wife	G	Jig
Humours of Westport	F	Reel		Micky Chewing Bubblegum	A	Polka
Hunter's Purse	a$_m$	Reel		Miss Johnson	G	Reel
Irish Washerwoman	G	Jig		Miss McLeod	G	Reel
Irishman's Heart to the Ladies	A	Jig		Miss Monaghan	D	Reel
Jackie Coleman's	D	Reel		Mist on the Mountain	a$_m$	Jig
Jackson's	D	Reel		Morning Dew	e$_m$	Reel
Jenny's Chickens	f#	Reel		Morrison's	e$_m$	Jig
Jessica's	A	Polka		Mountain Road	D	Reel
Jig of Slurs	De	Jig		Mountain Top	Bb	Hornpipe
Joe Cooley's	e	Reel		Moving Clouds	G	Reel
John Bowes	C	Reel		Mug of Brown Ale	a$_m$	Jig
John Brennan's	D	Reel		Mulvihill's	D	Reel
John Dwyer's	G	Reel		Munster Buttermilk	G	Jig
John Whelan's I & II	G/A	Polkas		Musical Priest	b	Reel
Johnnie Mickey's	A	Polka		Newmarket	A	Polka
Jordan Farm	F	Jig		Nine Points of Roguery	D	Reel
Julia Delaney	d	Reel		O'Keefe's	a$_m$	Slide
Kathleen Brennan	D	Reel		O'Rourkes	D	Reel
Keith Murphy	e	Reel		Off to California	G	Hornpipe
Kerry	D	Polka		Off She Goes	D	Slide
Kesh	G	Jig		Old Bush	a$_m$	Reel
Kid on the Mountain	e	Slip-jig		Old Grey Goose	e	Jig
Kildare Fancy	D	Hornpipe		Old Hag You Have Killed Me	G	Jig
Killarney Boys of Pleasure	e	Reel		Old Man Dillon	a$_m$	Jig
Killavel Fancy	G	Reel		Old Woman Tossed Up	A	Jig
Killavil Postman	D	Polka		Out on the Ocean	G	Jig
Killfodda	F	Reel		Over the Moor to Maggie	G	Reel
Kitty's Gone A-Milking	G	Reel		Paddy Clancy's	D	Jig
Kitty's Wedding	D	Hornpipe		Paddy Fahy's	g	Jig
Knotted Cord	a$_m$	Reel		Paddy O'Brien's	C	Hornpipe
Lad O'Beirne's	D	Jig		Paddy on the Railroad	D	Reel
Lady Ann Montgomery	D	Reel		Paddy on the Turnpike	g$_m$	Reel
Langstrom's Pony	A$_m$	Jig		Paddy's Trip to Scotland	D	Reel
Lannigan's Ball	e	Jig		Palm Sunday	a$_m$	Jig
Lark in the Morning	D	Jig		Parish	D	Slip-jig
Lark on the Strand	a$_m$	Jig		Patsy Geary's	D	Jig
Larry O'Gaff	G	Jig		Pay the Reckoning	G	Jig
Leather Away the Wattle,O	D	Polka		Peter Street	A	Reel

Tune	Key	Type
Pigeon on the Gate	e_m	Reel
Pinch of Snuff	D	Reel
Pipe on the Hob	D	Jig
Plains of Boyle	D	Hornpipe
Poppy Leaf	G	Hornpipe
Primrose Lass	G	Reel
Providence	D	Reel
Rakes of Clonmel	a_m	Jig
Rakes of Kildare	a_m	Jig
Rakish Paddy	D_m	Reel
Rambling Pitchfork I & II	D/e	Jigs
Ray's Favorite	a	Polka
Reconciliation	A	Hornpipe
Redican's	G	Reel
Reel of Mullinavat	e_m	Reel
Return to Miltown	Dd	Reel
Richard Brennan's	D	Jig
Richard's (1.42 lb. Check)	D	Polka
Rights of Man	e	Hornpipe
Road to Lisdoonvarna	e_m	Jig
Road to Rio	G	Reel
Rolling Waves	D	Jig
Rose in the Heather	D	Jig
Ryan's	D	Polka
Saddle the Pony	G	Jig
Sailor on the Rock	D	Reel
Salamanca	D	Reel
Sally Gardens	G	Reel
Scholar	D	Reel
Sean Ryan's I & II	a_m/a_m	Jigs
Sean Ryan's	G	Reel
Sgt. Early's Dream	dm	Reel
Shannon Bells	D	Jig
Shannon Breeze	D	Reel
Shaskeen	G	Reel
Sheehan's	G	Reel
Sheila Coyles	D	Reel
Ships are Sailing	e	Reel
Showman's Fancy	D	Hornpipe
Silver Spear	f	Reel
Silver Spire	G	Reel
Skylark	D	Reel
Slieve Russel	a_m	Jig
Sligo Maid	A_m	Reel
Smash the Windows	D	Jig
Snug in the Blanket	D	Jig
Spellan the Fiddler	G	Hornpipe
Sporting Pitchfork	G	Jig
Sporting Nell	D_m	Reel
St. Mary's/Church St.	G/G	Polkas
Stack of Barley	G	Hornpipe
Stack of Wheat	G	Hornpipe
Star of Munster	a_m	Reel
Stoney Steps	D	Reel
Swaggering	D_m	Slip-jig
Swallowtail	a_m	Reel
Swedish	DdD	Jig
Sweeney's	D	Polka
Sweeney's Dream	D	Reel
Sweeney's Wheel	b	Reel
Swinging on a Gate	G	Reel
Tam Lin	d	Reel
Tar Road to Sligo	D	Jig
Tarbolton	e	Reel
Tea Song	A	Jig
Tear the Calico	D	Reel
Tell Her I Am	G	Jig
Temperance	G	Reel
Tenpenny Bit	a_m	Jig
Tobin's Favorite	D	Jig
Tom Billy's	D	Reel
Tom Billy's	a_m	Jig
Tongs by the Fire	G	Jig
Top of Cork Road	D	Jig
Toss the Feathers	e	Reel
Touch Me if You Dare	G	Reel
Traveller	G	Reel
Trim the Velvet	G	Reel
Trip to Athlone	D	Jig
Trip to Durrow	D	Reel
Trip to Sligo	e	Jig
Tripping Upstairs	D	Jig
Walls of Liscarrol	D_m	Jig
West Clare	G	Jig
When Sick-Tea You Want?	D	Jig
Whinny Hills of Leitrum	b	Slip-jig
Willy Coleman's	G	Jig
Wise Maid	D	Reel
Woman of the House	G	Reel
Yellow Tinker	G	Reel

*Notation of Keys:

Upper case = Major

Lower case = Minor

Subscript$_m$ = Modal